If Germs Were Purple

Stanley L. Swartz

Illustrated by Steve Pileggi

Dominie Press, Inc.

If germs were purple,
I could see them.

I could see them
when I sneeze.

I could see them
on the sink.

I could see them
on the garbage can.

I could see them
on my teeth.

I could see them
on my hands.

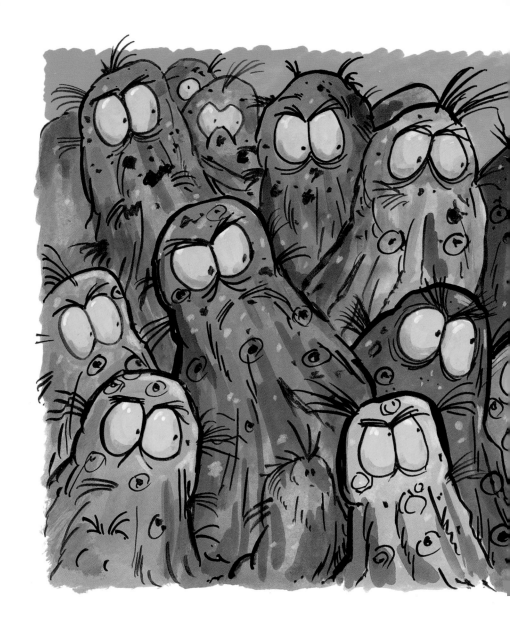

If germs were purple,

I would be more careful.

The development of the *Carousel Readers* was supported by the Reading Recovery project at California State University, San Bernardino. All authors' royalties from the sale of the *Carousel Readers* will be used to support various Reading Recovery projects.

Publisher: Raymond Yuen
Series Editor: Stanley L. Swartz
Editorial Assistant: Bob Rowland
Illustrator: Steve Pileggi
Layout: Michael Khoury

Published by:

 Dominie Press, Inc.
1949 Kellogg Avenue
Carlsbad, CA 92008 USA

ISBN 1-56270-861-9
Printed in Singapore by PH Productions Pte Ltd.
3 4 5 6 ITP 03 02 01 00

TITLES IN THE
Carousel Earlybird Readers Series

Carousel Earlybird Readers Set 1

The Bear
Big and Little
I Can See
I Get Tired
My Clothes
My Room
We Go to School
What Can I Read?
What is Red?
Where I Live
You

Carousel Earlybird Readers Set 2

Here Is...
I Am Thankful
I Can Draw
I Can Wash
Look at This
My House
The Sandwich
Things I Like to Do
This Game
What is Blue?
What's That?

Carousel Earlybird Readers Set 3

The Bouquet
Creepy Crawlies
Hair
I Can
We Ride
I Run
Lots of Toys
My Clothes
My Family
Salad
What is White?

Carousel Earlybird Readers Set 4

The Boat Trip
Find It
If Germs Were Purple
Pam and Sam At the Park
Pam and Sam At the Zoo
Pam and Sam Fly Over the City
Pam and Sam On the Beach
Signs
Things I Like
We Went Flying
What is Yellow?